THE SECRET BEHIND AMERICA'S MIGHT

Perhaps the Reason for 9-11

by

Chrispin Ntungo

Bloomington, IN      Milton Keynes, UK

authorHOUSE®

AuthorHouse™
1663 Liberty Drive, Suite 200
Bloomington, IN 47403
www.authorhouse.com
Phone: 1-800-839-8640

AuthorHouse™ UK Ltd.
500 Avebury Boulevard
Central Milton Keynes, MK9 2BE
www.authorhouse.co.uk
Phone: 08001974150

This book is a work of non-fiction. Unless otherwise noted, the author and the publisher make no explicit guarantees as to the accuracy of the information contained in this book and in some cases, names of people and places have been altered to protect their privacy.

First published by AuthorHouse 11/2/2006

ISBN: 1-4259-6519-9 (sc)

Library of Congress Control Number: 2006909313

Printed in the United States of America
Bloomington, Indiana

This book is printed on acid-free paper.

Dedication

To a world struggling to comprehend
America's might.

Acknowledgment

They did it. So, I thought I could do it too in my own way I could. Special thanks to American media icons, including Oprah Winfrey, Larry King, Paula Zahn, and the late Peter Jennings for their powerful shows, through which they have quietly and unknowingly inspired me through the years.

Table Of Contents

INTRODUCTION

America is undoubtedly the most powerful nation on the globe. The world knows it for its prosperity, media, and military might and proud citizens. Few, however, have taken time to discover the secret behind its might.

In *The Secret Behind America's Might* the writer "spills the beans," so to say, and presents what he has discovered to be the secret behind America's might.

The Secret Behind America's Might has sixteen stand alone and simply written, but very enlightening chapters, each speaking to one aspect of the secret. Most importantly, you will benefit from reading *The Secret Behind America's Might* if, once you understand the secret behind America's might, you can actually apply it to help yourself, and possibly your country, fulfill your dreams like most Americans fulfill their American dream.

The book's core message is universal. But Americans will certainly enjoy it most, especially if they don't mind sharing their secret with the rest of the world. Enjoy! TwCN.

CHAPTER 1

AMERICA, ONE BEAUTIFUL COUNTRY

America is one beautiful country strategically located between two oceans, the Atlantic Ocean on the east and the Pacific Ocean on the west. A beautiful country strategically located between two friendly neighbours, Canada in the north and Mexico in the south. I am from Zambia (Africa) a country located in the tropics that enjoys twelve months of sunshine annually. Now living in Canada a country of nine months of winter, a joke here, I look at America from a unique perspective.

When you hear us at Thursday with Chrispin Ntungo (TwCN), or anyone for that matter, describe America as beautiful, what comes to your mind? From our perspective, we think that there are two ways to describe the beauty of a country. The first is its natural environment, that is, the physical characteristics including landforms, climate, soils, and vegetation. The second is the result of human influence or development, often called culture. Our interest here is mainly in the natural environment. Basically we aim to point out how America is naturally well-endowed and how as a nation it has relentlessly exploited its natural resources for economic development and human advancement.

For once allow me to recall my high school geography. I attended high school in Zambia. One of my favourite subjects was geography. It was then that I learnt about North America, including Canada and the United States of America (U.S.A.). Generally speaking natural landforms, climate, soils, and vegetation have significant implication for human activity. There is no place where this is more so than America. In developing America, early settlers exploited the physical environment, including natural resources, for economic development. Economic activity dictated where new comers to America would settle and where cities would develop, and what type of economic activity would be predominant, whether it would be agricultural, mining, manufacturing, transportation or service.

In America, I see a country that has the best of all that nature offers, including physical characteristics such as landforms, climate, soils, vegetation and natural resources. Considering land features alone, America has all features but tropical rainforests. America has ice and snow, high barren areas, tundra and alpine, needle leaf trees or taiga, broadleaf trees, grasslands, dry scrub and desert. The northern part of mainland America, for example, experiences ice and snow. Ice and snow give American people the opportunity to enjoy winter activities and sports, including skiing, skating, and hockey.

Furthermore, in its northerly and farthest state Alaska (and I have been there by the way), America experiences the best of winters, if winter can ever be best. In addition, Alaska offers an abundance of natural resources, including wild life, oil, natural gas and minerals. While some people may consider Alaska as too remote and too cold, the American people in Alaska are mainly natives who are unique and have there own culture. Therefore, they are able to endure the winter, find ways to enjoy it and significantly contribute to the development of the state and America.

In contrast, the southern part of America offers the best that tropical weather has to offer. The region enjoys abundant sunshine allowing the people to grow fruits, enjoy life on beaches, and enjoy such sports as golf and athletics throughout the year. American countryside is one that I love to describe as gorgeous. Moving from east to west, I enjoy seeing the low coastal lands of the east, and moving over the array of a diverse landscape, including the Appalachian Mountains, the plains of mid America, the dessert in Colorado and the breath taking Rocky Mountains in the west part of the country. The landscape as described above is too simplistic in some ways. Geographers do a better job of describing it.

Interposing the American physical and natural environment with human activity, geographers have divided and described America in fourteen regions namely,

1 - Megalopolis
2 - Manufacturing Core
3 - Bypassed East
4 - Appalachia and the Ozarks
5 - Deep South
6 - Southern Coastlands
7 - Agricultural Core
8 - Great Plains and Prairies
9 - Empty Interior
10 - Southwest Border Area
11 - California
12 - North Pacific Coast
13 - Northlands
14 - Hawaii

It is not the intent of the writer to give a lecture on these regions, but rather to simply highlight how any kind of physical environment can be exploited and used for appropriate economic activity. Such economic activity needs to be encouraged and supported by government policy. And the American government has done a good job in ensuring that every part of America's natural endowment is economically utilized.

Much of the countryside is well developed. The Midwest is characterized by an extension of the prairies from Canada. Hence, it is a rich agricultural landscape with crops such as grain being predominant as well as food processing and manufacturing industries. The western and southern part of America is characterized by climate favourable to fruit production. Hence, it is rich in fruits and vegetables. In supermarkets you encounter such fruits as California oranges and grapes. The same is true for the sunny south like Florida where you find mainly Florida oranges.

The coastal areas are characterized by beaches that attract tourists from the interior of America as well as from around the world. These areas also have marine based industries such as fishing, fish processing plants and shipping.

You would think that because of the Rocky Mountains America would have a huge challenge balancing development between the east and the west. Far from it. The American government took the initiative years back and put in place amazing infrastructure that links the east and the west. The infrastructure includes a sophisticated highway network, railway lines and air transportation. Consequently, the natural environment coupled with human economic activity has made America amazingly beautiful making every individual American proud.

Deservedly so, the endowment of abundant natural resources coupled with well planned and coordinated human activity is indeed one secret behind America's might. TwCN.

CHAPTER 2

WAVE OF AWARENESS ABOUT AMERICA

Today, I hear about Presidents John F. Kennedy (in office 1961-1963) and Richard Nixon (in office 1969-1974). Since I was born in 1961, at the time these great Americans were presidents, I was too young to know anything about them. Moreover, I lived in a town called Mbala in Zambia where there was neither daily newspaper nor television (TV). But later in 1977, when I started attending secondary school, I became interested in radio as it was the only way to get news. It was then that I started hearing about a president of the United States by the name of James Earl Carter Jr. (Jimmy Carter), who was in office from 1977 to 1981.

Soon after Jimmy Carter, I began hearing about President Ronald Reagan. It was when Ronald Reagan was the president of the United States that I received all of my undergraduate university education (1982-1987). Before I was exposed to TV, I still remember once when the then President of the Republic of Zambia Kenneth David Kaunda visited the United States. And a Zambian reporter was reporting to Zambia from a Washington DC news bureau. The message was as clear as crystal and the quality of the news report was just phenomenal.

Later, I visited my cousin Captain Steven Sikazwe, an airline pilot, and he happened to have the Time magazine. I flipped through the pages and watched President Kaunda standing there at the White House with President Reagan. President Kaunda liked to wear grey safari suites and President Reagan liked black or navy blue suites. The two presidents together looked gorgeous as statesmen. I still carry that image today as an inspiration. That, in many ways, is what I describe for myself as the wave of awareness about America.

When I lived in Lusaka, Zambia, we used to watch on late TV a feature film program. It used to come right after the 10 P.M. news. My cousin Esther Nakazwe and I used to stay late for that program. And one day we were there watching the program when I saw this one character who looked like someone we knew. Then I said to my cousin, "That looks like Reagan." And my cousin said "Yes, he is Reagan." "He was an actor!," I exclaimed. And my cousin said, "Yea."

I love Americans. Only in America does anyone have equal chances to become a president. In many countries, ascending to the presidency is almost impossible. Imagine a circle and its centre. In many countries, the presidency is like the centre of the circle. And people in professions like acting are like right on the circumference of the circle. That shows you how far such people are from the centre of power.

But Americans are different. Americans would have actors for president over and over. Later in 2003, California would have elections for governor. And guess who would come into office to govern the great state of California? Arnold Schwarzenegger, another actor.

If you are honest enough, you can't help but admire Americans. They don't only do things differently, but they do them so well too. I hear some women going 'mmh that is not quite right.' The United Kingdom has had a female prime minister, India has had a female prime minister, Canada has had a female prime minister, but our country, and though you are so impressed by it, it has had no female president.

My thought is, yes, that is the nature of America. It is not that the opportunity is not there for a female to become president. But rather America still has to produce a woman who can stand firmly before Americans and lead them. Standing up means going through the ropes and chains and pangs that lead to the White House. It will never come on a silver plate. America by design as a country requires that you work your way to the office of the president. No one will ever do it for you. Corporate America has female presidents; and one day soon you can have hope that the country will have a female president too.

The idea that every American person who wishes to become president can actually become president is yet another secret behind America's might. TwCN.

CHAPTER 3

THE INFLUENTIAL PROFESSOR

As a young lad, I attended the University of Zambia from 1982 to 1987. It was common those days for developed countries to provide economic aid to developing countries. Some of the aid came in form of human resources or professional expertise. And so it happened that when I was in my fourth year, pursuing my first degree in agricultural sciences, one of my professors was Professor Snodgrass from New Mexico University on a USAID attachment to Zambia.

I wish I had a camera then, I would have taken a picture and, may be, included it here. Unfortunately, cameras were beyond reach especially of a student as I was. Anyway, Professor Snodgrass taught me Agricultural Production Economics. His face, the classroom setting and the notes he gave me and my classmates are still vivid in my mind. To this day, I still remember the famous decision point for production, MC=MR (that is, marginal cost equals marginal revenue). He was such an excellent professor.

Why am I telling you this story? Well, such are most American professors in most American universities.

Professor Snodgrass was just one in Zambia, what about all in America. Think about their collective influence on the quality of education in America. Think about the impact on the quality of graduates from American universities. To say the least, it is phenomenal.

In my native country Zambia, there is a saying that says *"Imiti ikula e mpanga,"* translated *"Trees that grow are the forest."* It is an undisputed fact that health trees result in health forests. Applied to education, it may as well mean kids that grow become the leaders of tomorrow. And with an excellent education system, this means people that are well educated will bring about a health vibrant economy, and hence, sustainable and significant economic development. The type of economic development as we see in America today.

Furthermore, America has numerous universities that have built excellent reputations for themselves. From the top of my head I can name the University of California at Berkley, Harvard, Stanford, John Hopkins, Texas MIT, and the list goes on. Most of these universities have produced graduates that have gone on to change the way business is done in America, gone on to make new discoveries and advances in science and technology, education and culture, and media and communications. From the opportunity I had of being taught by Professor Snodgrass, I could convincingly testify that American excellent professors help make America a mighty nation.

I have often seriously questioned myself, 'is this thought something that I just bear in my mind. How true is it that American professors are great?' Later, I attended the University of Manitoba, Canada, for my graduate education (1988-1991, 1993-1996). Being so close to the United States, I could not let the opportunity to attend conferences in America pass me by. So, on one occasion in 1995, I attended a conference in Indianapolis, Indiana, USA. I was very impressed at how Americans presented their papers. Most of them were confident, emphatic and clearly explained concepts and new findings.

Later on, when I returned to my school, I started to talk about how great American presenters were. To my surprise most people agreed with me. Visiting any library in the world today, I bet majority of books and journals that you will find are written by American professors and published in America.

Generally speaking, American teachers and professors, the people or the professionals, who speak to other people and transmit knowledge, do make a difference in building a country into a mighty nation. At TwCN we are convinced that yet another secret behind America's might is its fine professors and its fine educational system. TwCN.

CHAPTER 4

THE AMERICAN DREAM

T he American dream is a notion that the early settlers in America developed to inspire themselves towards achieving prosperity. It is the idea that it is only in America that if someone is intelligent enough and works hard he can achieve his dream of success and prosperity. And many Americans, who have believed in the American dream, have pursued their dreams. Through intelligence, hard work and some luck quite a number of Americans have become wealthy. The American dream was popularized by capitalists, including the famous Andrew Carnegie and John D. Rockefeller.

Not every American has been able to fulfill their dreams in America. But the most important question is, 'Does the American dream have any significance in turning America into a mighty nation?' We will answer this question properly. Imagine a country without any common goal for its citizens. Imagine a country full of citizens without any uniting aspiration. What would motivate its citizens to do anything with energy and life commitment? Likely your answer is nothing. And we concur with you.

Does the American dream have any significance in turning America into a mighty nation? Most people would say 'Yes' to answer this question. The notion of the American dream has served as an inspiring and motivating thought for majority of Americans. Since it is natural for a person to have aspirations or ambitions or goals in life, or a vision of one's future, the American dream serves America well as each of its citizens has embraced the concept and each one has believed that they are entitled to having a dream and working hard or smartly to fulfill it.

The consequence has been that as one American after another pursues their dreams; collectively they have united their initiative into a strong force for development of America. The American dream has served as a cultural norm for most Americans. American leaders needed not ask Americans to do anything other than reminding them saying you live in America, and America offers you the greatest gift, the gift of liberty to do anything within the law and to enjoy the fruits of your labour in the way you wish. And the majority of Americans, from one generation to another, have not been reluctant to exploit the opportunity presented to them.

Of course, we would be naïve to think that every

American has been able to achieve their dream. No doubt the American dream has not worked for everybody. However, our take is that it is still a necessary dream to have. Here is why we say so. Imagine 100 people having and pursuing the American dream. If 40 of these people achieve the dream, would you say the American dream does not work? We wouldn't say so. Forty people achieving the dream means forty people out of poverty, or forty people providing employment for the other sixty, etc. Contrast that to 100 people without a dream. The Good Book says that where there is no vision people perish. We can apply that adage here and say where 100 people have no dreams, nothing gets achieved. There is nothing to motivate these people. Hence there is unemployment, there is poverty. Of course, this sounds too simplistic since there is poverty in America too. But we trust you've gotten the message.

The American dream has done wonders for America, believe it or not. Once black Americans wondered if ever they would be totally liberated and ever earn the right to vote and have equal access to education and employment opportunities. Many had difficulty believing that they would ever live to enjoy American liberties and privileges. It took a younger preacher by the name of Martin Luther King, Jr. to passionately say, "I have a dream," to convince many black Americans that yes it was possible. The man rallied black Americans on the goal of achieving his dream of racial equality. And because he articulated it so well, people committed themselves to achieving that dream. Lo and behold it did not take long before they achieved it.

A lot of people who have come to America, instead of lazing around have been reminded to pursue their dreams. Some of these people heard about the American dream long before they moved to live in America. Others learn about the American dream when they are already in America.

Even though the American dream has its critics, you can't help but confess that it is a good reason to bring out the best in people. If there is power; if there is a force in individuals or societies having dreams, then the American dream has been a major force in inspiring Americans to develop as individuals, exploit their talents, accumulate lots of money, and consequently develop America itself into such a mighty nation that it is today. At TwCN, we don't doubt that the American Dream is yet another secret behind America's might. TwCN.

CHAPTER 5

RESPECT FOR EVERY ASPECT OF HUMAN ENDEAVOUR

I have traveled a little bit. At least I can say I have been to Africa, Europe and North America. There is no country where I have seen so much respect for every aspect of human life like in America. Aspects of human life, of course include such things as culture, technology, science, family, religion and business.

I grew up in Zambia. I recall as a young lad attending school. While in primary and secondary school, teachers and students respected those who were good at Math, English and Science. There was very little regard for individuals who were good in such subjects as music, home economics, history, and vernacular languages. Now, when I look back I kind of feel ashamed.

Americans have all aspects of human life well developed. And the foundation for development of every aspect of human life is respect. Respect for every type of activity and respect for every type of job. As a result, we see that an astronaut is equally respected as a movie star. An athlete is equally respected as a university professor. An elementary school teacher is equally respected as the President of a multinational corporation. And it makes sense. Basically, every aspect of human life is part of the complete whole. You can not advance in one aspect and lag behind in another, and call that development.

In terms of systems, the consequence is that the health system is just as important as the educational system. The public sector is just as important as the private sector. Children in day care are as important as elderly persons in personal care homes. What a society! For many a people coming from developing countries, America is light years ahead. There is no doubt that respect for every aspect of human life is critical to being a mighty nation. And for America, this is another secret behind its might.

In some developing countries, lack of respect for different aspects of human life is reflected in the wages and salaries that people who work get. In certain countries, it is unimaginable that someone whose work is focused on say enhancing or preserving culture would be rewarded the same as someone who is involved in developing engineering projects. It is perceived that engineering technology is more challenging, and therefore, more valuable than preserving culture. So a person involved in engineering technology is likely to be paid more than the person involved in culture.

But in America things are totally different. You can be a basketball or baseball player and make millions of dollars, in fact more millions than a doctor working from a local hospital. And amazingly, the basketball player will be equally respected as the doctor at a local hospital.

Where I grew up, things were totally different. Involvement in sports never took anyone anywhere. In fact, teachers had little respect for kids who were so good at sport and not so good in class. Somehow, and understandably so, because sports were not as rewarding as good grades in school. Looking back, what amazes me is that there was no one to change the situation and make sports as rewarding as academic achievement.

Oh America, if only you knew how wonderful you are, you would spend much time teaching others your way of life. That respect you have for every aspect of human endeavour is no doubt another secret behind America's might. TwCN.

CHAPTER 6

AMERICAN MEDIA FRENZY

If a question were asked, 'Which among the world's nations is the loudest nation?' chances are majority of people would say the United States of America. Why? Because of its media frenzy.

It does not matter where you are anywhere in the world, chances are you will be affected by the American media. American media includes local, national, and international television, newspapers, radio and magazines. And media is cultural in its influence. As millions of people from around the world feed on American media they become, unknowingly and unintentionally, Americanized.

Just think of the impact of American television. American television includes around the clock news channels such as Cable News Network (CNN) and national news channels such as ABC News, CBS News and NBC News. When you listen to these news channels you get to know more about what has happened in America and to the Americans within and without America.

Another interesting aspect of television is talk shows, including the ever popular Oprah Winfrey show, movies and late night shows. In as much as movies and talk shows are entertaining, they also have a lasting impact on people watching them. Over the years, my experience has been that I have increased in knowledge and intellectual capacity by learning. Learning happens by listening or reading and assimilating what I hear or read. I believe listening to TV news, movies and talk shows is, somehow, a way of learning.

As millions of people around the world listen and assimilate American news, movies or talk show discussions they educate themselves, though unknowingly, on American culture and its way of life. The subtle impact of this attachment to American TV is slow causing most people to yield to American culture. Often, it happens without knowing that as more people get accustomed to American culture, they slowly give up their own culture and make American culture supreme to theirs. In the long run, when we are all dead, Americans appear to be mightier than any other nation on the globe.

In addition to TV, there is American published news and magazines. In 1988, I made my way from Zambia to Canada. On my way, I passed through the United Kingdom (UK). Reading magazines is one of my passions. At London Heathrow, I took sometime to peruse through some magazines in news kiosks. I thought there were too many magazines. Then I arrived in Canada. As a student at the University of Manitoba, my favourite destination was not necessarily the library, but rather the bookstore. And inside the bookstore, the magazine rack. I couldn't believe how many magazines I saw. I spent countless hours perusing through the magazines. Overtime my favourite magazines became business magazines namely Forbes, Fortune, Business Week, and selected Fashion Magazines.

Once in a while, when I had the opportunity, I tried to explore subjects outside business and fashion, I discovered tones of more magazines. The majority of these magazines were American magazines. You wonder why I know so much about America today. It's because all I have known to read is American publications. Later on, I discovered there was Canadian Business, Manitoba Business and Profit magazines from Canada. But even then I did not find these as impactful as American magazines. I believe I am not alone in this trap. As a result, in my mind, and unfortunately in many people's minds American information, knowledge and way of thinking dominates. And because American information, knowledge and thinking dominate, it appears America is mightier than my own country. Such is the influence of the media.

To put the icing on the cake, so to say, American

laws have no restrictions on the media. As such American media range from the most holy to crap and in between you will find everything else. And people who come from nations where the media is not free, but rather controlled, when they get to America they want to feed on every restricted type of publication or TV program. And by so doing unknowingly Americanize themselves. The result is they give up some aspects of their culture to American culture and render America supreme. Yes, believe it or not, American media frenzy is yet another secret behind its might. TwCN.

CHAPTER 7

THE BEAUTIFUL FACES OF AMERICANS

It was lunch time at my place of work on a cold January day. What is better than the food you are eating at lunch in a deserted staff room where you are alone? Probably a fashion magazine, which happened to be there close by and I reached for it. Turning the pages, all I saw was one beautiful woman and another dressed in gorgeous attire. Then a thought crossed my mind, 'All these women are Americans.' "Aren't they beautiful?" I asked myself. It was then that I tried to put things in perspective. I couldn't help but to admit probably Americans have it all.

Just think about it, everywhere you look in America; on TV, magazines, movies, sports, music, theatre, news, shops, most of the people you will see are beautiful faces of Americans. It is the writer's biased opinion that Americans probably have the most beautiful women in the world.

Could it be the reason why American men are always happy and are prepared to do anything? Wake up men of the world and be reminded of one thing! There is probably nothing that moves the brain cells of a man than a beautiful woman on the side. There is nothing that moves a man to be an achiever than a beautiful woman on the side. There is nothing that makes a man defend whatever he has than a beautiful woman on the side. "Oh, he is out of his mind?" you think. Not quite. Isn't it true that naturally women motivate men? And American men are possibly the most motivated in the world. Is it any wonder that there are so many American dream makers and achievers?

If the world was fair likely everyone would confess that American women are beautiful. Why is it that women celebrities are always beautiful and gorgeous? Why is it that men celebrities always have a gorgeous American woman on the side? Think about it. You must be convinced that Americans know the secret that motivates men and they strongly believe that they have it.

You may have heard about Vietnamese Americans. You know the greatest punishment you can give an American man is to separate him from his beautiful woman. This is what happened during the Vietnamese war. American marines were for the longest time separated from their beautiful women. To find a way out they ended up dating Vietnamese women. But the relationships were not the same as American men experienced dating there own women. Why would TwCN say that? Listen!

American women are probably the happiest of all women in the world. At TwCN we love the way American women express themselves. They are totally liberated, totally free. When they speak, they speak with their entire minds and from the bottom of their hearts. They can tell you what they need and when they need it and from whom they need it. What kind of woman do you think makes a man an achiever? Believe it or not it is the most liberated woman. And American men seem to get the best that any woman can give a man. No wonder their men appear so pleased and at ease radiating the fact that they have it all.

Contrast that with the marines that went to war in Iraq. For religio-cultural reasons Americans would not date Iraqi women. No Iraqi woman who had never been exposed to America would agree to date an American marine. As a result, American marines likely found it very frustrating to serve in Iraq. One wonders whether that frustration showed most when they had the opportunity to abuse the Iraqi captives of war. You probably know the story.

The beautiful faces of Americans, you can't help but admire them. It is tempting to say that if the world was observant enough everyone would treat women like the Americans do. And the women would give the very best to their men and their communities. Consequently, everyone would enjoy life like the Americans enjoy it.

At TwCN we enjoy putting all kinds of thoughts across. As a result, chances are we can easily be misunderstood. And in this instance we are not saying that everyway American women are treated is the best. Far from it! The bottom line, however, is that American faces are beautiful; and the faces of American women simply gorgeous. Join us in admiring them.

There is an adage that says 'behind every successful man there is a woman.' It, therefore, appears that behind the success of every American man and the mightiness of America as a nation, there is that gorgeous, well liberated yet loving and caring American woman. TwCN.

CHAPTER 8

A NATION ON ITS KNEES

Oh my God! Is what you will likely hear when you watch America's award giving events such as country or pop music awards or movie Oscar awards. "God Bless America" is likely what you will hear from any elected American official. It's a virtue of most, if not all, Americans.

Summer of 1997, I was driving on Highway No. 2 traveling from Winnipeg, Manitoba to Detroit, Michigan. It was a Sunday. And like most travelers, the radio was my best companion. Being Sunday morning, every station I tuned to in Minnesota, Wisconsin and Michigan, I found a religious service on. And I listened intently. The preachers preached, and their "flocks" sung praises to God Almighty. Then I got myself thinking. Which country on earth is so open about religion as America? Which country on earth offers so much liberty to its nationals so they can each worship according to the dictates of their conscience? Of course, I thought about Canada, the United Kingdom, Zambia, the countries with which am most familiar. Of course, there is freedom in these countries, but if we were to rank them, chances are America would rank first.

America is one country I call a nation on its knees. Its leaders know how to pray and they know the power of prayer. They may not show it publicly. But surely they know how to exclaim "God Bless America" in public. This expression is like patented or copyrighted. Other leaders, like those in Canada or Zambia can't even say "God Bless Canada" or "God Bless Zambia" for it does not sound real. It appears like they are just copying American leaders; and the expressions don't appear to carry any power in them. But when an American leader says "God Bless America" everyone is able to recognize that there is power in that expression, in that prayer. Majority of Americans feel America is a blessed country. You can see it in the way they worship, with conviction and power.

A story is told of two astronauts, one an American and the other a Soviet Unionist (from those days). When the Soviet Union astronaut went into space he exclaimed, "I don't see any god up here." But when the American astronaut was asked, "What do you see?" he said, "I see the mighty power of God." Majority if not all Americans believe in the power of God and his providences. American leaders know for sure that America as a nation is a favoured nation and a nation blessed by

God. And wise leaders within the majority of American leadership have inquired, why of all the nations did God choose to bless America? The answer lies in the values that America is built on and espouses. Simply put, so that America can be leader in bringing freedom to many of the world's captives. People in other lands who have no freedom of expression, freedom of worship, freedom of choosing their leaders, freedom of enterprise and the rule of law. No wonder America is a superpower today. You see, America's superiority is no accident.

For sometime, I used to be bothered a great deal, when I heard of there being Chaplains for the American Senate and American service men. Now I understand. By and large, Americans are strong believers in God. From experience they know that as humans there is no inner strength without God. American decision makers and American service men need that inner strength to be able to achieve what they set their minds to. And so they ensure that they have someone to provide spiritual guidance. It is not any wonder that most, if not all American leaders, have the Good Book on their office shelves, and most, if not all, American service men have the Good Book in their back packs. It is the book to read if they are to get wisdom and strength to serve from one day to another. It is an excellent strategy and it works effectively.

At TwCN we really believe America is a country on its knees. And its prayers to God, its fear of God and its claim on God's promises is yet another secret behind America's might. TwCN.

CHAPTER 9

AND THAT LIBERTY

Whether I live in the slams of New York or Johannesburg, whether I live in the mountains of Afghanistan or the sands of Iraq, or whether I live in the ice lands of Canada or the waters of Hawaii, just give me that liberty, leave me alone and see what I can do. Liberty! The liberty to think and speak freely; the liberty to worship according to the dictates of my conscience or the liberty to move as I wish, or the liberty to associate with whoever I want. Just give me that liberty and wait and see what I can do.

Americans are likely the most liberated people that have dwelt on earth. Their freed minds allow them to think and speak on issues freely; to write and share ideas freely; and to invent and try things freely. The result of that liberty has been phenomenal. It made the difference between the fall of communism and the victory of democracy. It made the difference between those who constantly walk in Africa and those who constantly fly in America.

Growing up in Zambia from the early 1960s way up to my university years in the 1980s, I grew up under the one party rule of President Kenneth Kaunda. Kaunda espoused humanism, an aspect of communism or socialism, as his philosophy for social and economic development. Under humanism the law of the land did not allow anyone to be on his or her own. Those who worked lived in either a city council or a central government house. If they drove cars, they drove either a government owned company car or a government department's car. No one was allowed to own any property. If you were heard talking about anything against the government or government official you risked disappearing and no one would know how. You were deprived of liberty. Someone thought for you and you simply followed someone's directives. Policy makers were called Members of the Central Committee (MCC). Everything revolved around and was on the peripheral of this inner circle central committee.

As a result, there was no economic development for almost twenty-five years. By the time the people of Zambia embraced democracy and its liberties early 1990s, the country's economy had already been brought down on its knees, so to say; broken to almost beyond repair. Zambia is just one example here. Many other African countries followed the same path and denied their people that liberty, the liberty that America has enjoyed from its beginning. The liberty that is indeed another secret, in fact, a backbone of the secret behind America's might.

If you are a leader of a developing country and you want your country to develop, try giving your people that liberty. Try giving them the freedom to do whatever they want as long as they don't infringe on each other's rights, you will be amazed what your people are capable of achieving.

The world has embraced so much of American culture. This is so for a very simple reason. Everything seems to begin and flourish in America simply because in America everyone has the liberty to try their idea. And new ideas are welcome as opportunities for prosperity. They are welcome as opportunities for fulfilling each individual's American Dream.

People always amaze me when I bring up the concept of the greatest prison. Most people will tell you, the greatest prison is one like the Americans built for Taliban and al Qaeda prisoners at Guantanamo Bay, Cuba. Close. But I always argue that the greatest prison is a situation or condition or kind of society that takes away my liberties. By and large that is what most prisons do. And some nations, unfortunately, are more prison than countries.

Ask any American senator or congressman. Ask any American media person from Larry King to Oprah Winfrey. Ask any American athlete or business person. Ask any American student or professor; ask any American church minister or movie actor, ask any credible world leader, chances are, they will all say yes, liberty is another secret behind America's might. TwCN.

CHAPTER 10

NO AMATEURS FOR PRESIDENT

You can never be a President of America if your leadership skills have never been proven before. You see, the American political system is such that the executive leadership is trained and tested long before it gets to lead from the White House. Every American citizen, and this is probably arguable, can ascend to the presidency. But there is a process.

The United States of America is a union of fifty states. The fifty states form an excellent training ground for most individuals who would be presidents in America. States are headed by Governors. At any given time, America has 50 governors. It is a pool of experienced leaders each of whom has equal opportunities to ascend to the presidency. The issues that state governors deal with at state level provide them with experience and confidence to run America as President. It is in this case that no American president is an amateur.

The alternative to having governors ascend to the presidency is having vice presidents or senators or congressmen ascend to the presidency. By and large, vice-presidents, senators and congressmen are also familiar with many issues that the executive deals with. And if candidates are well connected with the people they usually do have the opportunity to become presidents.

In some countries around the world, people rise to the presidency without having any past leadership experience. This is more so true in developing countries where people as simple as a Sergeant in the army can rise to the presidency through the barrel of a gun. From where on earth did a sergeant get experience to lead a country challenged with economic and social problems? Bet you me no where.

In order to achieve sustainable development, it is prudent to have well experienced, well educated people become presidents. America has it and its performance in terms of development shows. Believe it or not, there is no doubt that having no amateur presidents is yet another secret behind America's might. TwCN.

CHAPTER 11

ILLEGAL IMMIGRATION

No one disputes that America is a country built through hard labour. From the early years the country utilized slave labour to enhance its economic development. Today, America boasts of having officially put an end to slavery. Oh! Thank God.

But seriously speaking if slavery were classified into hard and soft slavery, some slavery would still be identified as still existing in America today. Let us begin by distinguishing between hard and soft slavery. Let us agree that hard slavery is one like when people were forced to work in agricultural fields under the scotching sun for hours and hours without compensation. Compare that with soft slavery where people are indebted and live in poverty doing mediocre jobs and paid only the minimum wage. If this distinction is accepted, chances are soft slavery still exists in America today, unfortunately.

When it comes to immigration America can be credited for its objective selection of immigrants.

The country seeks and encourages anyone with a remarkable talent or skill to join and become one of its people. As a country, America provides tremendous development opportunities in every area of human endeavour. As long as you have an immense talent, whether it is intellectual or physical talent and/or skill, America welcomes you to develop your talent and/or skill within its boundaries. Over the years America has reaped tremendous benefits from legal immigration that brings in new talent and skilled people. Legal immigration allows you to have a green card, a magic card that gives you rights and privileges to legally work in America and be gainfully compensated.

However, over the years America has also seen an increase in illegal immigration. Illegal immigrants and workers are individuals who do not have the green card, yet they are still able to work, but illegally in America. Do authorities know that there are such people in America? Of course, they do. And this is where it becomes interesting. By and large authorities know, but they let them stay and work anyway. Why? is perhaps another of your questions.

When I studied economics, first at the University of Zambia and later at the University of Manitoba, I learned that the common objective of firms is to maximize the difference between sales and expenses. For every item produced or service rendered, there is a human expense, in addition to other expenses, associated with it either while still in production or during the sale. As a result one of the major expenses firms face is the human expense. Therefore, if a firm can find a way to reduce the cost of labour, the likelihood that the firm would increase the difference between sales and expenses, commonly called profit.

American businesses know the value of illegal immigration. They have tremendously benefited from it by employing illegal immigrants and paying them minimum wages, but not any medical insurance or pension benefits. Illegal immigrants know this is a Catch 22 situation for them. If they speak out, they risk being deported, and if they stick around they risk going without a job. And authorities know that there are illegal immigrants in the country, but as long as they are contributing to the economy and helping boosting productivity at low costs, the better. As long as they don't involve themselves in crime and/or we don't catch them they can stay.

Zambia, my native country, got its independence in 1964. At that time its neighbours Angola, Namibia, Zimbabwe (Rhodesia then), Mozambique and South Africa were still under colonial rule. A good number of nationals of these countries came to live in Zambia. Today, I imagine that if Zambia had put those nationals on Zambian farms or in Zambian firms and paid them minimum wage, Zambia would have benefited tremendously economically. But Zambia never did that as its motive was to genuinely assist its neighbours win independence from colonial rule. This example may appear to be out of context. But don't worry. It serves only one purpose; to paint a picture depicting how aliens can benefit a country, and how in America, aliens continue to benefit America today.

Over the years, the contribution of illegal immigrants to the American economy has been tremendous. And at TwCN, not mentioning slavery, we believe that profiting from illegal immigrant labour is yet another secret behind America's might. TwCN.

CHAPTER 12

PARTNERING WITH THE POWERFUL

America salutes her allies, all the time. The likes of the United Kingdom, Canada, Germany, Japan, South Korea, China, France and Italy are equally powerful or influential. And America is quick to seek partnership with them when it needs them. Looking at the nature of conflicts America is involved in, one can't help but exclaim what America probably thinks: 'we shall smack the weak, but we shall partner with the powerful doing so!' This is foreign policy in its own class.

In strategic literature, this may as well be called aiming at protecting national interests. You see, the American leadership has all kinds of cards in its arsenal of strategic decisions. America treats with respect countries that are rich in black gold, commonly called oil, or that are located strategically in relation to supposed American enemies. Rather than engage in foreign policy that does not benefit America, the American leadership simply keeps a low profile. But for countries that have black gold, or oil, America is quick to extend its hand of friendship.

For this reason, some people say that America has double standards. But Americans know that this is just another secret behind America's might. Why send your troops to die in alien lands that would never benefit you in any way? It does not make sense. There must be a good reason for risking the lives of American service men in alien lands.

You see, America is probably the only country that has options when it comes to acting on the international scene or world stage. For something that's significantly beneficial to America alone, America has the ability to go alone. But it also has options to go with the North Atlantic Treaty Organization (NATO) or the United Nations (UN). For something that is not significantly beneficial to America, America is quick to suggest sending the United Nations to do the job. For something that's significantly beneficial to Western Europe and North America, America has the option to go with NATO. How many countries in the world today have such options? Only one, that is, the United States of America.

The ability to be able to stand alone or to partner with the powerful on the world scene may appear to be ineligible, but it is yet another secret behind America's might. TwCN.

CHAPTER 13

THE REAL SECRET BEHIND AMERICA'S MIGHT

If you are open minded and mindful of the welfare of your people, at the very least, you can't help it but admire the United States of America's presidential debate. Listening to the American presidential candidates debate, is a rare opportunity for learning about democracy, learning about values, learning about conviction, learning about faith, learning about building bridges and learning about what to value in your personal life.

It was interesting to watch George W. Bush and Kerry Edwards battle it out in the presidential debates leading up to American presidential elections on November 2, 2004. But does it matter what the American presidential candidates debate on? Does it matter who finally ends up in the White House?

It is human nature to take sides. When you take

sides, you follow the debate closely and subsequent analysis by the media. You feel affected. You feel scratched on one side or the other. Inevitably you want to wish victory for one of the two candidates. In this sense you would say that it matters what American presidential candidates debate. But the irony is that unless you are an American you have no control, you are just an outsider looking in.

What do you do when there are certain things about either candidate that you like? You know that the White House can only take one president. It is at this point that you start thinking, well, it does not matter who finally ends up in the White House. Whether the democrat or the republican ends up in the White House, for many of us it would still be the same old world. We would still face the same challenges we have known over the years.

What then is the value of American presidential debate to those of us outside America, and especially those coming out of developing countries? During the debate, you couldn't help but admire the clarity in identifying issues to debate on. Such issues as education, jobs, health, immigration, environment, etc. You couldn't help but admire the fearlessness of the candidates. Candidates debated while being sure that after the debate they would go home safe and secure without fear of being harassed by any elements of the opposition. Candidates debated believing that the campaign playing field was level and that the election process was transparent.

At the end of the debate, you couldn't help but to admire how the candidates shook their hands. You couldn't help but to admire how the two candidates hugged each other's wife. You couldn't help but to admire how the candidates were surrounded by their families with no ill feelings from the audience. And you couldn't help but to ask, 'Why can't other societies, especially those in developing countries do the same?' America, indeed, has something to offer the world. Arguably not everything, but sure America leads when it comes to tolerance, peace and freedom. America could be and is a school for many who dream to be free and prosperous. But who would learn from America when what comes to mind first is meanness towards her.

It appears that the secret behind America's might lies not in what people know America for – wealth, money, movies and a powerful military, but rather in the ability of leaders and their followers with opposing views to respect their differences, tolerate one another, unite in peace and freedom and fight the common enemy. And the common enemy is not one armed with weapons of war; rather it is hunger, disease, poverty, unemployment, and illiteracy. America has long defeated the common enemy. Consequently, freedom and prosperity have followed. It is this freedom and prosperity that attracts people to America.

Every time you see opportunities for improvement, your heart must go out to Africa and her people. You see, the people of Africa have so much in form of dreams. But Africans still have to overcome the common enemy. This may not happen until African leaders have renewed minds and learn from the American school to practice the values of tolerance of opposing views, respect for independent opinion, and promote peace and freedom for their people.

Lastly, it does not hurt to make you know that over the years, one of the hardest things we have learned at TwCN is to give credit where it is due. And we have learned, though some may argue otherwise, that for certain things America deserves credit. And some of these things are, in fact, yet another secret behind America's might. TwCN.

CHAPTER 14

INFLUENCE OF HEROES, STARS, SUPERSTARS AND ROLE MODELS

Early 2005, I had the privilege of visiting America. It was snowy and in the twenties below zero when I left Winnipeg, Canada for Savannah, Georgia, United States of America (USA). When I arrived in Savannah, it was nicely warm and totally opposite of what I left in Winnipeg. Indeed, it wasn't a bad place to spend a week.

Reason for visiting Savannah

My trip was strictly a business trip. So I had the opportunity to meet and mingle with Americans at work. We were about 480 professionals in all. But I could count less than ten blacks, three east Indians, two Orientals and the rest were whites. This observation got me thinking - I must be really privileged to be part of this profession; or this profession must be well protected; or may be it is a profession not so well marketed to ethnic groups.

The profession is that of International Association of Assessing Officers and Urban and Regional Information Systems Association. Members of these two associations include property assessors, appraisers, and geographic information systems specialists. The industry itself is huge. To give you an idea of how huge this industry is, think of all the fifty states in the USA and the ten provinces of Canada. Think of all the cities in these states and provinces. Then think of all the real estate, commercial and farm properties in these cities. They number in the hundreds of millions. All these properties have to be appraised for tax purposes. Entry requirements include a bachelor's degree including some training in (urban) economics and statistics.

Learning from sessions

I attended and evaluated a number of sessions. Overall, only two presentations met my stringent criteria for international conference worthy presentation. My stringent criteria were partly because of my background in academics. But it is here where I thought I had a lot new to learn.

I think that America is a wonderful place to be and it is a wonderful model for any developing society. As an overseas African, to have the guts to make any presentation, I usually want to make sure that what I present is no less than perfect. Perhaps it must be critiqued by those I highly respect. And if they suggest that it is not worthy to be heard by anybody that likely is the end of it. No more presentation. But it appears that in America that is not the case.

To me Americans seem to have this philosophy - any idea or any experience or any thought is worthy sharing. As well, any question is worthy asking and no question, whatsoever, is a foolish question. And so when Americans meet they allow anything to go, that is, to be presented and heard. After hearing, then those who see the opportunity sift through the information and build on the foundation that has been laid. No wonder although the first people to go into space were Soviets, the winners of the space race were Americans.

Ideas pursued by the bold few

Many Americans have ideas, but only the few bold ones are able to pursue their ideas. It is these few that become heroes, or stars, or superstars or role models. The rest of the society emulates these few. Just think of television (TV). America is a country of 240 million people. Of all these people, no more than 500 are famous characters on TV as sports stars, movie stars, news reporters, or politicians. It is these people that you see on TV day-in and day-out. You never get tired hearing about them in newspapers and magazines or watching them on TV. But these few people have so much impact on the lives of Americans and to some extent the lives of people elsewhere around the world. It is the accomplishments of these few that make all Americans so proud. And because of them every American walks with his or her head up and speaks loudly and proudly. Some observers say Americans are stubborn. But don't let the alleged "stubbornness" of Americans prevent you from learning from them or stifle your creativity and your determination to be successful and prosperous. As long as you respect freedom of speech and individuality, you are welcome in their ranks.

I observed on one hand, as one after another of American appraisal professionals spoke, they were bold and courageous, and they joked too. I also observed on the other hand, that even when the presentation was not up to the calibre I expected, the audience provided opportunity for the speaker to present his or her ideas and experiences, and they listened intently and asked questions or provided positive comments. Somehow, I thought to myself, these people live in a developed country. But their development did not come over night nor was it a smooth road. Rather, it was by trial and error, building on one idea and another until the outcome was perfected. I also thought that these people are clever, they write down everything so that they don't have to re-invent the wheel over and over. More importantly, where one leaves off, the other takes over and builds on.

I knew it was because of my background that I thought like I did. When some of the presenters gave a brief history of their city or state, they talked of how their cities began in the 1800s. Having come from Zambia, I couldn't help but to think that Zambia was "born" in 1964 so that today, it is only 40 years old while most US states and cities are hundreds of years old. And by and large Zambian development is not totally from within; rather it is a copy cat kind of development. That means, looking to England or America and trying to have what they have. Rather than encouraging self actualization and nurturing own development ideas and developing policies and programs through which such ideas can mature and produce fruits, freedom of enterprise is stifled. With no original ideas, ideas that you can control and be proud of, it should be pretty hard to achieve sustainable development. And this is true for most African countries.

TV away from home

From the streets of Savannah into my hotel room, I thought I would turn on the TV and see what I saw on the streets. Far from it. I found TV terribly boring. It was the same kind of channels and same characters as I see from Canada.

You see when western journalists go to continents like Africa, they visit lowdown areas and take videos and pictures of poor neighbourhoods and children, and bring these and show them on TV in the West. The rest of the western society sees these pictures and believe that this is Africa and its culture. Terrible misrepresentation!

The same is true with what we see on TV in North America. TV shows very little, but it is such a powerful medium that every one believes it reflects society. What North American TV highlights are what are popularly known as role models or superstars. As well, TV shows heroes. At any rate, these are not typically the norm for society. But the rest of the society emulates these people and over time the accomplishments of these stars is reflected in society as a whole.

Ending

All in all, it appears that another secret behind America's might is the ability of its citizens to follow in the footsteps of their heroes, role models, stars and superstars. These heroes, role models, stars and superstars are in all fields of human endeavour (not only sports and music) but also academics, medicine, business, politics, science and technology. TwCN.

CHAPTER 15

A PREACHER'S IDEA ABOUT THE SECRET BEHIND AMERICA'S MIGHT

L eft to a preacher of the Good News the mightiness of the United States of America is foretold by the Creator in the light shining in the dark place of the Good Book. According to the preacher when the Good Book's light shining in the dark place is carefully studied and well expounded the symbols used in the Good Book have meaning. The symbols include waters, beasts, horns, land and wind. Using the Good Book as its own expounder, symbols have meaning vis-à-vis waters represent people, beasts represent kingdoms or nations, land represents empty places and winds represent strife or war.

The preacher reads a verse in Revelation 13 that speaks of another beast like a lamb coming up out of the earth; and having two horns. The preacher expounds saying the beast like a lamb represents a nation which comes into existence around 1798 AD. One horn on the beast represents political liberty and the other horn represents religious liberty. Putting the two together, a picture separating church and state is painted. This is what America is known for, clear separation of church and state.

Reminding his audience of the middle ages, the preacher expounds further saying the Christian church, which was concentrated in Europe, was fiercely persecuted during the period from 538 AD to 1798 AD. The persecution went on unchecked partly because Church and State then were united and operated as one. The Church made rules and through the State enforced those rules using the Courts of the Inquisition. Those who went contrary to the rules were subjected to punishment, which was fierce persecution.

As persecution prevailed for over a period of 1,260 years, the preacher says the Creator answered the prayers of the saints and paved a way to their freedom. That way saw many believers leave Europe for America. When these believers arrived in America and established a government they did not want to have a similar form of government as existed in Europe. So they established a government with clear principles that separated the State from the Church. They also granted total religious liberty to citizens allowing them to worship according to the dictates of their conscience. It was during this time that the famous Statue of Liberty in New York was erected. The Statue of Liberty is a special monument to remind future generations of Americans of the liberty that was achieved when those who escaped persecution in Europe found freedom in America.

The American settlers, who established the American government, were most enlightened. They used their enlightenment wisely and established the best constitution on the globe. In addition to making a clear distinction between Church and State, they also granted other freedoms as are known today under the banner of democracy and human rights.

The preacher, however, does not stop sharing the light shining in the dark place without warning. He warns that this same America that was founded on the principles of the Creator will eventually compromise its principles of liberty. It will take away some of the liberties and help bring people to conditions such as those experienced during the middle ages. He warns everyone to watch out.

In closing, the preacher establishes a bottom line. No matter what happens in the future, the preacher says the bottom line is that another secret behind America's might is that America is a nation that was foretold, raised by and blessed of the Creator. TwCN.

CHAPTER 16

WHAT WOULD AN AMERICAN DIE FOR?

At the core of this book, I have tried to share with you, in a somewhat humorous and intriguing way, what a true American believes in. When I shared the idea of this book with the publisher, he wrote to me and said:

"I am intrigued by the book that focuses on American values and Americans' desire to export the best things we offer—personal freedom, creativity, industry, and Democracy—to the rest of the world. As a student of history I am aware that there has long been a tendency in the American character to share the fruits of our prosperity and social stability with those who could benefit most. This is often lost in the recent focus on the negatives of globalization and corporate politics. Such a book can provide an important stimulus to this generation, and help others around the world to take advantage of opportunities this instinct offers."
— Dan Heise.

"American values," those are the two words I was looking for. I deliberately avoided using them in the earlier chapters in fear of turning you off completing to read this book. Dan alluded to them in the above paragraph. Americans use them with pride, but the rest of much of the world hears them with a sense of scorn. And it is not that the values in themselves are awful, far from it. But I believe it is because of the way, or the process by which, Americans bring them to the attention of the world. If American values are so important to humanity, and indeed they are, then they need not be called American values. Rather call them something that reflects the fact that they are *humanity's universal values for pursuit and experience of happiness.* And for the sake of argument, allow me to call them *humanity's universal values for pursuit and experience of happiness.*

Yes, America has embraced *humanity's universal values for pursuit and experience of happiness* and has benefited immensely from them. If properly taught and shared with other people around the world, there is no doubt that humanity would benefit from them.

Another point I wish to make is that Americans use the term self-interest and actually put self-interest first when dealing with outsiders. And it is the image of self-interest first that does not rest well with most outsiders, the non-Americans.

I owe it to you to answer the question 'What would an American die for?' It is my opinion that an American would die for *humanity's universal values for pursuit and experience of happiness.* These values include the power to generate wealth or Capitalism, Democracy and Personal and Religious Freedom. These values are ingrained in the American history and the Americans' belief in their county's future. In my world these are the cornerstone values on which American might is built.

Other values are simply versions of or hinge on these cornerstone values. These values include equality, independence, individualism, faith, family, wealth, happiness, rule of law, creativity, helper of the oppressed, defender against tyranny, manifest of destiny and personal privacy. You can see that as you introduce versions and versions of the cornerstone values, conflicts occur. But thank goodness the conflicts do not in any way render the values powerless or meaningless. Rather, these versions of cornerstone values clearly express and show where within the human spectrum of life they apply.

Lastly, I should make it very clear that every human being would enjoy living these values. As it is seen in the world today, if individuals don't experience these values in their own countries, cities, towns and villages around the world, they seek to move to America, and when they do that they demonstrate that America has something beautiful to offer the world. This something beautiful or *humanity's universal values for pursuit and experience of happiness* is the secret behind America's might and is undoubtedly what an American would die for. TwCN.

KINDLY MEET THE AUTHOR OF THIS BOOK

Chrispin Ntungo was born at his grandfather Kawa (William) Ntungo Simukwanya's village by River Mwame, in Mbala, Zambia, Africa on November 4, 1961. People called the village William after his grandfather's English name.

Chrispin attended Mbala Government School from 1970 to 1976 and Isoka Secondary School from 1977 to 1981. He was admitted to the University of Zambia School of Agricultural Sciences in November 1982. He completed his Bachelor of Agricultural Sciences degree in July 1987 after which he accepted a Training Instructor position at the Natural Resources Development College in Lusaka, Zambia.

In April 1988, Chrispin was retained by the University of Zambia as a Staff Development Fellow. He pursued his Master's degree in Agribusiness

Management from 1988 to 1991 at the University of Manitoba. After achieving his master's degree he worked as a Lecturer at the University of Zambia during 1992. In January 1993, he returned to the University of Manitoba to pursue his doctorate degree in Agricultural Economics, which he achieved in October 1996.

Chrispin met the sweetheart of his life Grace Kamanga at the University of Zambia in 1992. The two were married on August 8, 1993 in Lusaka and have since been blessed with four children Myazwe, Mbawemi, Chawezi and Mutende.

Since 2003, Chrispin is dedicated to writing and training to inspire, motivate and empower individuals to recognize and exploit their potential while achieving their goals. He founded Thursday with Chrispin Ntungo (TwCN) in 2003. The popularity of TwCN articles speaks volumes to their practicality and relevance. Consequently, Chrispin is a published author of *Well Disciplined To Excel (2005), Influence for Positive Change (2006)* and *The Secret Behind America's Might (2006).* At the time of publishing this book Chrispin worked as Acting Manager of Quality Services at the City of Winnipeg Property Assessment Department. TwCN.

To order this book or other of Dr. Chrispin Ntungo's books contact:

By Phone:	**1-888-280-7715**
My Mail:	**AuthorHouse,**
	1663 Liberty Drive,
	Suite 200,
	Bloomington, IN 47403.
Internet:	**www.authorhouse.com**